**Evariste KANYINDA**

**Identification system based on RFID technology**

AF209946

**Evariste KANYINDA**

# Identification system based on RFID technology

**Identification and control based on RFID technology "the case of the Marist University of the Congo" UMC**

**ScienciaScripts**

Cover image: www.ingimage.com

This book is a translation from the original published under ISBN 978-620-2-54961-5.

Publisher:
Sciencia Scripts
is a trademark of
Dodo Books Indian Ocean Ltd. and OmniScriptum S.R.L publishing group

120 High Road, East Finchley, London, N2 9ED, United Kingdom
Str. Armeneasca 28/1, office 1, Chisinau MD-2012, Republic of Moldova, Europe
Managing Directors: Ieva Konstantinova, Victoria Ursu
info@omniscriptum.com

Printed at: see last page
**ISBN: 978-620-3-26969-7**

## GENERAL INTRODUCTION

Technology is present in our lives and will continue to amaze us with the quality and speed of its functions. They improve our lives through the amount of information open to all, they inform about everything that is happening around the world, they guide us in decision making and allow us to update ourselves easily. In education, it has always been a concern for humans to identify, locate and track objects using first visual identification and then replaced by electronic equipment. Several practical systems have been used over the years, unique patterns have been placed on objects, and recognition devices could identify these codes and by the same token the object on which they are stuck. From this was born the barcode system which, for several years, made the dream of object identification a reality. However, barcodes have several shortcomings, including the lack of data storage, the need to scan them at a distance of a few meters, etc... These deficiencies have continually pushed mankind to search for a better solution to overcome this lack, and this is why RFID technology was born, which a priori solved the major problems of identification, localization, tracking and data analysis.

# TABLE OF CONTENTS

# PROBLEMS

Nowadays, checking the presence of agents in a workplace can be a complicated task because of the number of agents that can be considerably high. This can become even more complex if there are several departments. In this work, we are interested in the development of an intelligent on-board identification and control system based on RFID technology.

## OBJECTIVES
## GENERAL OBJECTIVES

The main objective of this work is twofold:

1. First, the presentation of a theory on RFID and Arduino technologies;
2. Secondly, the development of an intelligent on-board identification and control system based on RFID technology.

## SPECIFIC OBJECTIVES

In pursuing this research, we have set ourselves the following goal:

- To propose a solution that will guarantee the quality of service in the field of attendance verification.

## CHOICE AND INTEREST OF THE SUBJECT

In spite of a certain potential in the expansion of information technologies, the niche of verification systems still seems to be under-exploited in the Democratic Republic of Congo and more particularly in the city of Kisangani by the actors of the professional world. Spontaneously, the first explanatory factor evoked is that the management of an attendance verification system requires a certain amount of administration, time and financial means. It is clear that generally, during working hours, there are delays that occur when certain control operations are carried out. Thus, this research has allowed us to acquire sufficient notions for the development of applications integrating embedded system technologies. Moreover, it has allowed us to understand cards with RFID transponders and to use them to facilitate certain events in our daily lives. In dealing with this search term, motivation and personal interest also come from the fact that companies will find here a solution such that, assuming that each agent has a card with an RFID transponder, the proposed system should assist human resources departments in the automatic registration of attendance and in the control of agents and the time they spend at work.

## RESEARCH METHODOLOGY AND TECHNIQUE

### METHODS

We use the following methods to identify all the issues related to our work: ➢ Descriptive method: it consists in describing, naming or characterizing a phenomenon, a situation or an event so that it appears familiar; thanks to this method, the understanding of the functioning of information technologies and the description of the existing in the field of study are made possible to us.

### TECHNIQUES

For the realization of this research, we used the documentary technique: it allowed us to carry out a review of the literature related to our research. It also allowed us to be in contact with books, journals, course notes, articles and various publications resulting from the webography in order to dress our research by supporting it with value arguments.

### SUBJECT DELIMITATION

As the focus of this research is the development of an intelligent on-board identification and control system based on RFID technology, we are marking our boundaries in the context of a company seeking to relativize the time its employees spend at their workstations. Our goal is not to develop an application comparable to the complex verification and monitoring systems existing under other skies, but above all to prototype the verification system in order to make the most of it.

### SUBDIVISION OF WORK

Apart from the introduction and the general conclusion, this work is divided into four chapters divided as follows:

- Chapter I. General information on RFID technology ;
- Chapter II. Presentation of the UMC (study environment);
- CHAPTER III. Concepts About On-Board Systems ;
- Chapter IV. Implementation of the Automatic Pointing System

## CHAPTER I. GENERAL INFORMATION ON RFID TECHNOLOGY ;
## 1.1 INTRODUCTION

RFID (Radio Frequency Identification) technology is in full development. Equipped with a fixed or mobile transmitter, a receiver in the form of an antenna and a chip (one or more) called a tag. This type of communication by radio wave makes it possible to make an almost instantaneous survey of several chips. Thus one has access to an identification of an object, its tracking, these characteristics and one can even follow its path. We find them in :

- A parcel tracking system ;
- An animal identification system ;
- A library management system, etc...

This technology faces several constraints including cost, simultaneous reading management, and reading through different materials of different thicknesses. The term RFID (Radio Frequency Identification) encompasses all technologies that use radio waves to automatically identify objects or people. An RFID system is generally composed of a reader and a marker (radio tag). The reader emits continuously an electromagnetic field and by entering in the periphery of this field the label provided with a chip delivers its information to us through its antenna. The RFID technology has contributed in a consequent way to the improvement of the automated systems in detection and traceability. Often compared to the bar codes, the RFID also allows us the scan and the identification of the objects. But the comparison stops there because the use of the electromagnetic waves instead of an optical reader allows us to cover a larger space and to detect several elements at the same time, and this in the presence or not of an obstacle or any materials between the reader and the label; which is a saving of time and efforts not negligible for the user. The RFID system is a very attractive technology for the companies, it offers them the possibility of an automatic management of the consequent number of information which they must treat. The equipment adapted to this system makes it possible to synchronize the physical flows with the flows of information.

## 1.2 OPERATION OF THE RFID

A complete system using RFID technology is composed of the following elements:

- A transponder: or label that is programmed with data identifying the object on which it will be placed;

- An antenna: which is generally integrated into the RFID reader and the RFID tag. It makes it possible to activate the tags in order to receive data and to transmit information;
- A reader: fixed or portable, which is an essential element in the use of RFID. It transmits through radio waves the energy to the RFID tag, a request for information is then emitted to the RFID tags located in its magnetic field, then it receives the answers and transmits them to the concerned applications ;
- The RFID software: or RFID middleware, is the brain of the RFID chain. It makes it possible to transform the raw data emitted by the RFID chip into comprehensible information, it is of course managed by a computer. Figure 1.1 illustrates the elements composing the RFID system:

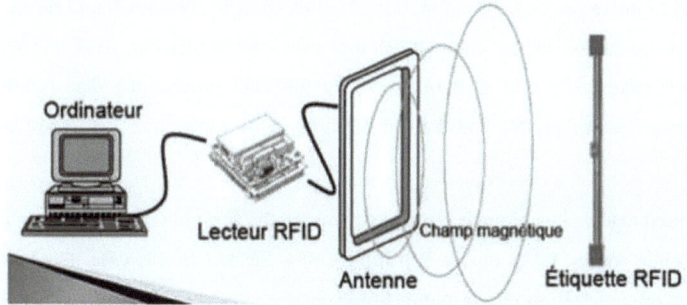

Figure 1.1 - Illustration of an RFID system

## 1.3   EVOLUTION OF RFID TECHNOLOGY

RFID was a technology developed by the army during World War II, its use coupled with the radar had for objective to identify the aircraft in flight ("Friend or Foe" long range identification system). The project was for a while reserved for sensitive sites such as military bases or nuclear power plants. At the beginning of the eighties, RFID tags started to be manufactured by several European and American companies and during the following years the RFID technology spread in the private sector and in particular in agriculture for the identification of cattle. In 1990 "IBM" took the initiative to miniaturize the RFID system by integrating it into a single electric chip, thanks to which the 2000s saw a boom in applications and an unprecedented exploitation of this technology. In 2003 the US non-profit entity EPCglobal, a joint venture between EAN International and the US Uniform Code Council (UCC), created the EPC standard (Electronic Product Code - an international coding system for the unique identification of all goods in the supply chain). The EPC standard integrates RFID and Internet technologies to set up the traceability network of objects.

RFID technology is now widespread in virtually every organization involving automated systems, and has spread to both the industrial and public sectors.

## 1.4 THE DIFFERENT COMPONENTS OF A RFID SYSTEM

### 1.4.1 RFID DRIVE

The RFID reader is a set of fixed or mobile equipment, consisting essentially of an antenna and an RF module. As soon as the tag is in the action zone of the reader, an energy is supplied to the tag so that it can function. It sends specific commands and receives in return information contained in the chip. In another case, the reader can read and write, so the information received is sent to another device that will process the data (computer). The frequencies used are variable and depend on the type of application. There are two types of readers:

- Fixed reader: it is mounted in a fixed way, in the form of terminals or gantries ;
- Mobile reader: takes on the appearance of a flasher. In this case it is the reader that moves so there is no need to move the tag.

The choice of a reader is very important. It varies according to the frequency of use and the power (field of action).

### 1.4.2 THE RFID TAG

The RFID tag is an electronic circuit that includes a chip and an antenna and responds to commands issued by the reader. There are two categories: active and passive. The active tag supplies its own energy through a battery, the passive converts the received signal into energy to be used for transmission.

### 1.5. ALLOCATED FREQUENCIES

The RFID system uses the hertzian channel for its communications. It must thus respect some regulations. The RFID standard is the subject of studies which aim at determining standards of radio frequencies emission (a range dedicated to the RFID system), this range of frequency is of type ISM (Industrial Scientific Medical frequency range)[1]. They are thus classified into four categories:

- LF : for frequencies below 135 MHz ;
- HF : For frequencies around 135 MHz ;
- UHF: For frequencies around 434 MHz, 869-915 MHz, 2.45 GHz ;
- SHF : For frequencies around 2.45 GHz ;

  Figure 1.2 shows the breakdown of the regions (as well as a table) that highlights the different frequencies allocated :

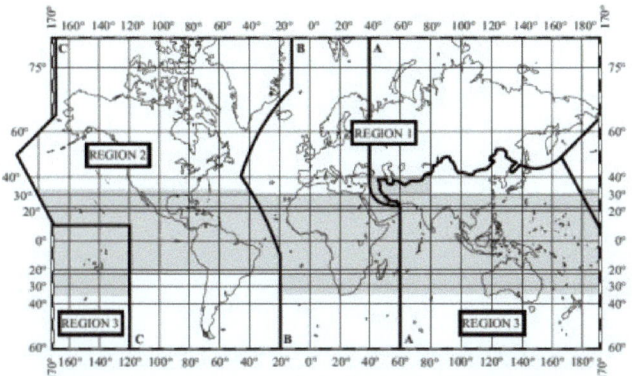

Figure 1.2 - ISM Frequency Allocation for RFID Technology

| Frequencies | Region 1 | Region 2 | Region 3 |
|---|---|---|---|
| BF | <135 KHz | <135 KHz | <135 KHz |
| RF | 13.56 MHz | 13.56 MHz | 13.56 MHz |
| UHF | 865.5-869.65 MHz | 902-928 MHz | 860-960 MHZ |
| Microwave | 2.4-2.4835 GHz | 2.4-2.4835 GHz | 2.4-2.4835 GHz |

Table 1.1 - Frequency Allocation

## 1.6 TAG TYPES

## 1.6.1 ACTIVE TAG

---

[1] *Jean-Ferdinand Susini Hervé Chabanne, Pascal Urien. RFID and the Internet of Things, Hermes Science Publications, 2010.*

Its power supply comes from an internal source in the form of a battery, cell, etc. This can effectively increase the range of the signal and thus communicate with a low-powered type of player and at distances of about 20 to 100 meters[2] . The main advantage of this type of tag lies in the fact that the tag does not have to be close to the reader.

Figure 1.3 - Active RFID Tag

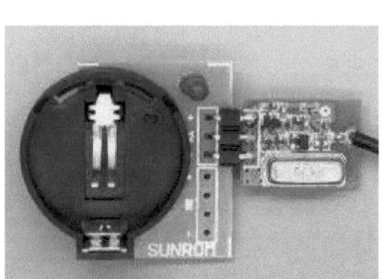

**1.6.2 PASSIVE TAG**

Compared to the active tag, the passive tag is less expensive and can be smaller in size. When the tag receives an electromagnetic signal, it stores energy in an on-board capacitor [3]and this process is called inductive coupling. When the capacitor is sufficiently charged, it powers the tag circuit which in turn transmits a modulated signal to the receiver (reader) that includes information contained in the tag. The communication between the two devices uses two methods to modulate the signal to be transmitted. Two other methods of classification of the RFID tags were: read-only (RO) and read/write (RW).

[2] *Joe Carr Steve Winder. RFID a guide to radio frequency identification. Newnes, 2002.*
[3] *idem*

The RO type is characterized by a memory that can only be read. It can be assimilated to barcodes because of its static memory. Thus the latter cannot be altered, this type is frequently programmed with a limited amount of static data to store a serial number or identification number for example[4]. The RW type also called "Smart", more handy than the RO tags can store a large amount of data with an addressable memory that can be easily modified, the data can be changed or erased as many times as desired. Thus some Tags are equipped with both RO and RW memory types at the same time. For example, the RFID tag of a pallet has a serial number contained in the RO section of the memory for the entire duration of its use and the RW section can be used to indicate the content at any time and when the merchandise is renewed or changed; this section of the memory is rewritten to follow the change of the content.

Figure 1.4 - Passive RFID Tag Compared to a Grain of Rice

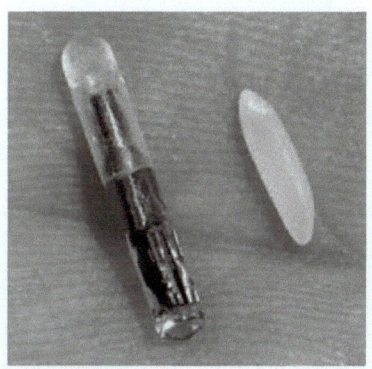

### 1.7 RFID STANDARDS AND NORMS

A standard is a reference document approved by a recognized standards institute such as AFNOR. It defines characteristics and voluntary rules applicable to activities. It is the consensus between all the stakeholders in a market or sector of activity.

A standard makes it possible to :

- To define a common language between economic actors: producers, users and consumers ;
- Define the level of quality, safety and least environmental impact of products, services and practices;

[4] *Jean-Ferdinand Susini Hervé Chabanne, Pascal Urien. RFID and the Internet of Things, Hermes Science Publications, 2010.*

- To harmonize good practices.

The standard facilitates trade, both national and international, and helps to better structure the economy and make life easier for everyone. Unlike a regulation, a standard is voluntary: compliance with it is not an obligation, but a commitment by companies to meet a recognized and approved level of quality and safety.

The fields covered by the standards are as varied as the economic activities and also affect RFID, and two organizations are presented that support the standardization of RFID systems: ISO and EPCGlobal.

### 1.7.1 THE EPCGLOBAL STANDARD

The EPCGlobal consortium was born from the cooperation of the MIT and GS1 Auto-ID labs (known for the creation of the EAN format). It is interested in the development and establishment of standards for electronic labels, electronic product codes and the EPCGlobal architecture. It was created with the goal of developing the use of electronic labels worldwide and integrating them into a global system. Several axes have been developed in this direction.

- Create low-cost electronic labels: labels affixed by a manufacturer on a product are not returned to him.
- These tags must operate in Ultra High Frequency (UHF) to have good physical properties (allowing a reading distance for example) and make the RFID system global in order to make it possible to use the labels affixed to the products at each intermediary (see scenario).
- Create a network architecture so that anyone can access the information associated with a serial number stored on a label.

These last two points highlight the need for interoperability (see issues) and are therefore based on open standards.

The EPC (Electronic Product Code) network is an architecture of standardized and open interfaces, designed to support better visibility of the location and movement of objects in production lines; with granularity down to the unique EPC identifier of each.

Unlike ISO, the consortium is composed of industrial (Cisco System, Sony Corporation, DHL Solutions Innovations among others), academic (MIT), or non-profit organizations (GS1).

The EPCglobal standard consists of :

1. A sequential product coding system, the Electronic Product Code (EPC).
2. Of a standard of RFID label, hierarchized in 4 classes :

   Class 1: single-read-only epc labels

   Class 2: additional features :

   Read/write, data security,

   Theft detection

   Class 3: class 2 + battery

   Class 4: stand-alone RFID relay

## 1.7.2 STANDARD ISO (INTERNATIONAL ORGANIZATION FOR STANDARDS

The International Organization for Standardization (ISO) has written standards for the identification and management of objects or equipment in the ISO 18000-x series of interface protocols designed for logistics operations. These standards cover the entire range of frequencies used worldwide for RFID. The seven elements of this standard are as follows:

- 18000-1: Radio Frequency Identification (RFID) for object management - Part 1: Reference architecture and definition of parameters to be standardized.
- 18000-2: Radio frequency identification (RFID) for object management - Part 2: Communication parameters of a radio interface below 135 kHz.
- 18000-3: Radio frequency identification (RFID) for object management - Part 3: 13,56 MHz radio interface communication parameters
- 18000-4: Radio Frequency Identification (RFID) for Object Management - Part 4: 2.45 GHz interface communication parameters.
- 18000-5 : Radio interface protocol for RFID systems operating at 5.8 GHz. The purpose of this standard was to define the physical layer, the anti-collision system and the values of the RFID protocols operated in the 5.8 to 5.9 GHz band. This topic of standardization was abandoned due to a general lack of interest.

- 18000-6: Radio frequency identification (RFID) for object management - Part 6: Communication parameters of a radio interface between 860 MHz and 960 MHz.
- 18000-7: Radio interface communication parameters for passive RFID systems operating at 433 MHz.

The most important of these standards for high frequency RFID is ISO 18000-6C. The corresponding protocol was prepared by "GS1 EPCglobal" and is often referred to as the "EPC Gen 2 standard". EPCglobal is also the author of an HF EPC standard based on ISO 18000-3. ISO 15693 refers to the radio interface of high-frequency tags whose protocol is read at less than 0.9 meters. These labels are used in inventories of pharmaceutical products and, more generally, small objects. ISO 14443 also refers to a protocol used on a high-frequency radio interface that is read from a short distance. It is mainly used for secure financial transactions.

## 1.8 APPLICATIONS OF RFID

RFID is currently a fast-growing technology that is developing in increasingly varied fields; security, transport, logistics, customer loyalty, payment, health, etc. Its use varies according to the frequency (LF, HF, UHF) where each frequency range meets a standard that describes a series of RFID technologies (ISO 18000-x) as we can see in the following examples :

| FREQUENCY | APPLICATIONS |
|---|---|
| <135 kHz | -Waste sorting,<br>-Animal identification (134.2 kHz),<br>-Alarm system, surveillance of trees in Paris . |
| 13.56 MHz | -Contactless smart cards, transport cards...<br>-Airline ticket booking, baggage handling<br>-Ski resort package . |
| 443 and 900MHz | -Tracing of pallets, containers,<br>-Centralized opening remote controls |
| 2.45 and 5.8 GHz | -Toll booth,<br>-Automatic fuel delivery at service stations. |

Table 1.2 - RFID applications according to frequencies

## 1.9 CONCLUSION

This chapter provides an overview of RFID technology. This technology makes it possible to collect information without having the tag in visual, to modify these data, to carry out several readings... So many advantages that it brings in comparison with other technologies such as the bar code. Admittedly this technology is in full expansion, it is put forward in the commercial sector but its applications are colossal: taking the medical field where RFID is under development, whether for identification and localization of patients, personnel, infants or surgical equipment and instruments. Despite the strong regulation of the healthcare sector, legislative changes in favor of RFID in the USA have contributed greatly to its adoption, estimating the RFID market in this industry at approximately $2.4 billion with a growth rate of 29.9%. [5]

---

[5] *RFID system for sensor reading; ISO 15693, 13.56MHz. HES-SO Valais-Wallis, institute of microtechnology IMT; University of Neuchâtel.*

# CHAPTER II: PRESENTATION OF THE UMC

The objective of this chapter is to present what exists in the research community. Throughout this phase, we will briefly introduce the research community and then outline the preliminary expression of needs.

## II.1. HISTORY

The Congregation of the Marist Brothers of the Schools (FMS) arrived in the Democratic Republic of Congo on September 7, 1911 to take care of the official elementary school for boys. It received from the colonial authorities of the Belgian Congo the mission to settle in the Oriental Province. It was in Stanley town, today Kisangani, that the Marist Brothers opened their first school in the Belgian Congo.

The year 2011 was an important turning point in the mission and life of the Congregation of the Marist Brothers of the Schools in the DRC. The celebration of the Centenary of the Marist work in the Congo was an occasion for an evaluation of the past and a projection for the future.

To mark the end of the first centenary of the Marist presence in the Congo and the beginning of the second centenary, the Marist Brothers of the DRC, meeting in a Regional Assembly in Kisangani, at Christmas 2010, decided to erect an educational work that would constitute a monument offered to the Congolese youth in general and to that of the Oriental Province in particular today, the Province of Tshopo.

The feasibility studies for this educational work were entrusted to a group of three Brothers, namely Brothers Masumbuko Mununguri, Médard Lusuna Mwana Kyomba and Valentin Djawu Lungumbu Wambo. At the end of a process of survey and exchanges, it emerged that there was a clear desire to launch a university rather than a higher institute.

Steps were taken to obtain the necessary authorizations from the National Ministry of Higher and University Education.

In August 2011, the Ministry of Higher and University Education issued a decree authorizing the Congregation of the Marist Brothers of the Province of East Central Africa to open a private university in Kisangani, Orientale Province, DRC, under the name "Université Mariste du Congo (UMC). »

The Organizing Power of the brand new university set up a team composed of brothers and laypeople to prepare for the effective opening of the Marist University of the Congo.

The launching of the activities of this University took place in 2012 with the opening of the first academic year 2012-2013 on October 13, 2012 and the inauguration ceremony of this University took place on April 20, 2013 in Kisangani. The Marist University of Congo is thus in its third year of operation.

## II.2. GEOGRAPHICAL LOCATION

The Marist University of Congo is located between the road leading from Bangboka International Airport and Mobutu Boulevard known as Camp Ketele Road. It is bounded to the North by the Mwangaza Primary School, to the South by the Mwangaza Teachers' Camp, to the East by the Kabondo General Reference Hospital and to the West by the Sainte Marie School Group.

In the commercial district, Commune Makiso. It is located in the former installations of the Champagnat Institute Boarding School in the city of Kisangani, Oriental Province, in the Democratic Republic of Congo. Thus, the Marist University of the Congo is located on the Internat of Mwangaza in the Commercial District, Commune Makiso, in the city of Kisangani in the DRC.

## II.3. UMC'S OBJECTIVES

Like all universities in the world, the UMC is open to all those who would like to deepen their knowledge of the world, society and their environment. While promoting Christian values, the UMC proposes to ensure the integral formation of the human being in order to help him or her contribute effectively to the construction of a human and fraternal world.

The adequacy between knowledge, reason, faith, science and love constitutes the foundation on which the Marist University of the Congo is building its educational system. The programs of the National Education offer the material to achieve this harmonization between scientific knowledge and the daily life of the populations that the

17

Marist University of the Congo is committed to introducing into the modern world, made of justice and peace.

The Marist University of the Congo is an institution that has a vision, a mission, that conveys certain values and that puts in place the means to achieve its vision and mission

## II.4. VISION OF THE MARIST UNIVERSITY OF CONGO

With its Marist pedagogical approach bequeathed by Saint Marcellin Champagnat Founder of the Marist Brothers of the Schools, the Marist University of the Congo wants to be an institution of reference to contribute to the regeneration of the human and social capital destroyed by anti-values.

## II.5. MISSION OF THE UMC

The mission of the Marist University of the Congo is to evangelize by Christianly educating young people in an integral and pluralistic approach so that they become virtuous citizens in :

- Providing training for design executives in various areas of national life through the teaching of subjects in the official curriculum in order to promote the blossoming of new ideas and the development of professional skills;
- Contributing to the evolution of science through the organization of basic and applied scientific research, oriented towards the solution of the problems that arise in the Oriental Province in particular and in the country in general; but also taking into account the evolution of the world;
- Helping the regeneration of human and social capital, destroyed by anti-values, according to the Marist pedagogical approach;
- Forming a world citizen, an entrepreneur, a person of value capable of understanding and solving problems in his environment.

## II.6. VALUES CONVEYED BY THE UMC

In order to form good citizens and virtuous Christians, the UMC trains in the following values:

- Love of a job well done

Manifested through discipline, effort and honesty. Today, with the "law of least effort" revealed through anti-values such as corruption, tribalism, regionalism, influence peddling due to belonging to a political party or a certain social rank, neglect, laziness, relativism, favoritism, etc., it is possible to see how this law of least effort can be applied to the people. The Marist University of the Congo wants to instill love, honesty and effort for a job well done.

- Equal opportunities for all

Achieved through justice, fairness and love. For "to educate young people, we must love them all equally," Father Champagnat used to say.

- Setting an example

To be an educator is a responsibility that requires a continuous presence and to be more witness than teacher .

- Simplicity

Our relationships, our encounters with others must be simple and regenerative. This is the pedagogy of "begetting" dear to our Lord Jesus: "I have come that you may have life and have it in abundance. "(Jann 10:10; Is 62).

- Family spirit

Lived by practicing respect, solidarity, sense of responsibility and co-responsibility. I am because we are the Marist University of the Congo. Knowing how to live, knowing how to live with others.

## II.7. MEANS USED BY THE UMC TO ACHIEVE ITS VISION AND MISSION

The means used by the UMC to achieve its vision and mission are :

- Peace education

In a country and a world in perpetual turbulence creating conflicts of all kinds and wars, the Marist University of the Congo wants to train peacemakers by organizing a peace education department within the Faculty of Psychology and Educational Sciences.

- Language learning

Being part of a globalized world, the Marist University of the Congo teaches English, Spanish, Portuguese, Arabic and Chinese to its students in order to know and understand the culture of other peoples and the global village.

- Entrepreneurship

In view of the number of unemployed and literate people and the employment policy in our society/city and since "We are in the process of moving from a society of managers to a society of entrepreneurs" (John Naisbitt), the Marist University of the Congo, through its pedagogy, wants to encourage the emergence and development of the spirit and entrepreneurial capacity of each student in order to be useful to him/herself and to society.

- Marist pedagogy

Like Mary Mother of Jesus, Model of the Marist educator, the UMC is attentive, listening to young people in order to help them discover the best of themselves, to encourage them through their experiences to become responsible for their lives and thus take charge of themselves.

## II.8. ORGANIZATION AND OPERATION OF VARIOUS SERVICES

Since the Marist University of the Congo is an organization, we choose to describe its functioning according to the theory of business organization of Hermes. Indeed, according to this thinker, any organization must assume four main functions: the management function, the distribution function, the production function and the logistics function. But before going into detail about these functions at the UMC, it is useful to present the organization chart of this organization.

## II.9. ORGANIZATION

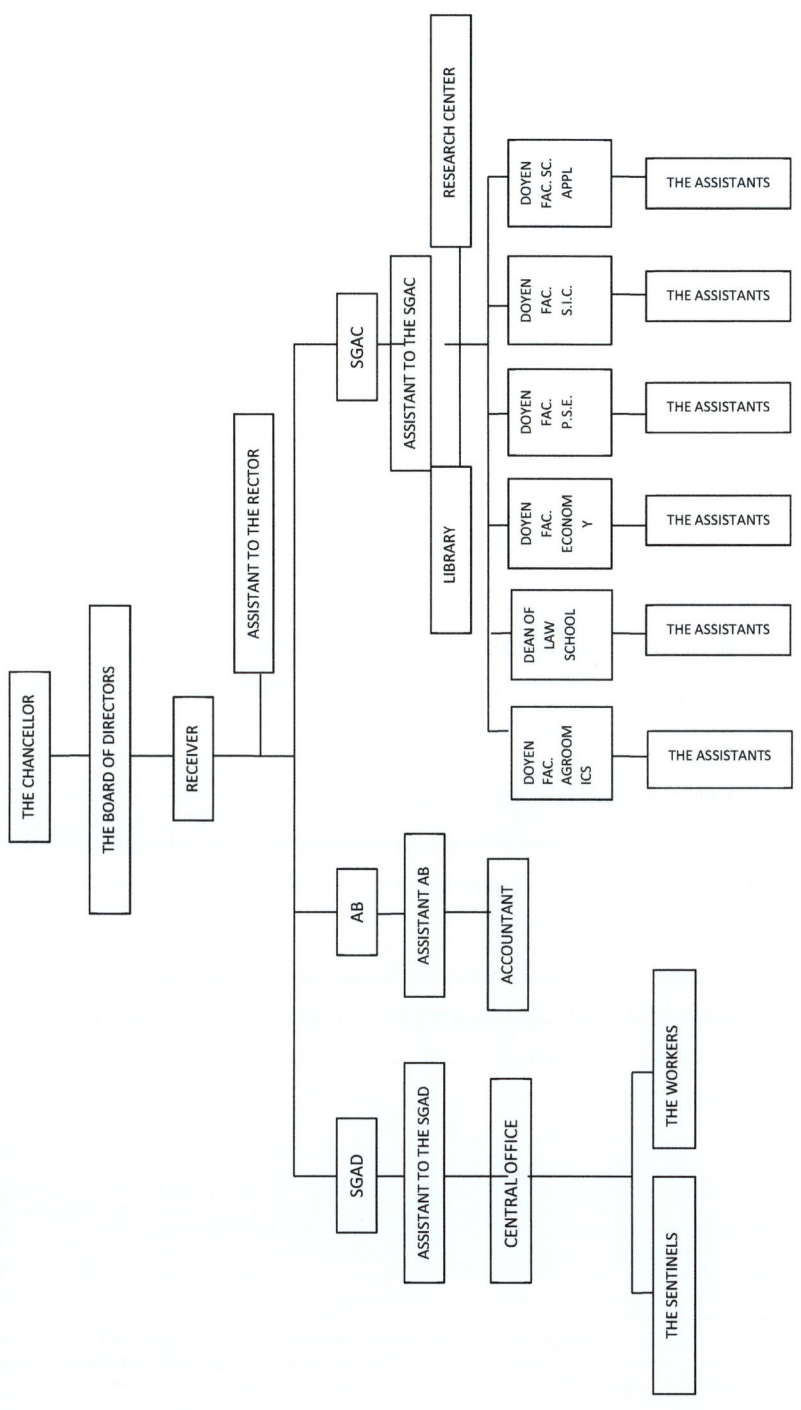

## II.10. STUDY OF THE EXISTING SITUATION

### II.10.1. PRELIMINARY STUDY

New Information and Communication Technologies (NICTs) have changed our daily life. Cars, airplanes, trains, satellites, cell phones, gates and doors, homes, ... nothing that communicates or moves can do so without electronics and electromagnetic waves informs Capgemini Consulting in the article Impact of new information and communication technologies on the quality of life and health at work. [6]

In this part, we will present the basics of the representation of the system needs to be realized. The exercise will consist in organizing our thinking to contextualize and understand the scope of the problem we are trying to solve. The main objective of this preliminary study is to establish an initial collection (or specifications) of functional, operational and technical needs.

To conduct our research, we used a participatory approach that advocates active involvement on our part and which enabled us to identify the following: employee attendance in  this institution is manual and poses enormous problems for the human resources department to control exactly the arrival and departure times of each worker.

### II.10.2. CRITICISM OF THE EXISTING

As mentioned above, there is no automated help system that directly collects the arrival and departure times of employees at the CMU. It follows from this that there is no criticism to be made in this regard.

For the future and in relation to the objectives we have set ourselves, the system we are going to develop is a new system and has no reference with any functioning of S. I as it does not exist. The system that we propose here is therefore only the result of innovative analyses and reflections.

---

[6] *Capgemini Consulting, "Impact of New Information and Communication Technologies on Quality of Life and Health at Work," [Online]. Available:https://www.fr.capgemini-consulting.com/resource-fileaccess/resource/pdf/impacts_des_ntic_sur_la_qualite_de_vie_et_la_sante_au_travail.pdf.*

## II.10.3. PROPOSED SOLUTION
### II.10.3.1. A QUID SOLUTION?

In a simple way, is called solution, everything that ends a problem. In IT, a solution is a software approach dedicated to a resource management problem. [7]

Given the current consideration and evolution of information technology, we postulate that a Computerized Attendance Verification System could be of valuable assistance in assisting supervisors with automatic attendance recording.

### II.10.3.2. SPECIFICATIONS

What are specifications?

A specifications document is a contractual document describing what is expected from the project owner by the project manager. It is therefore a document describing as precisely as possible, with simple vocabulary, the needs to be met by the project owner. Insofar as only the prime contractor is really competent to propose an appropriate technical solution, the specifications should preferably show the need in a functional manner, independently of any technical solution, unless the technical environment in which the requested solution is to be inserted is specified. [8]

### II.10.3.3. PRESENTATION OF THE PROJECT

In order to allow a fluidity in the process of checking the presence of employees, the thought comes to use a system that allows to know exactly the arrival and departure times of each employee.

The system is intended to contain data related to the different flows related to attendance at the workplace. The goal remains and remains that of creating a tool to assist in the verification of presence.

---

[7]     lintern@ute,     "Dictionnaire     Fraincais     Solution,"     [Online].     Available: http://www.linternaute.com/dictionnaire/fr/definition/solution/#definition.
8 CCM, "Cahier des charges," April 2017. [Online]. Available: http://www.commentcamarche.net/contents/978-cahier-des-charges.

## II.11. PARTIAL CONCLUSION

In this part, we have just briefly explored the research environment and the study of what exists in it. The study of the existing being the first phase of the unified process, the purpose of this part was to introduce us to the clarification of our investigation.

# CHAPTER III. CONCEPTS OF ON-BOARD SYSTEMS
## III.1. INTRODUCTION

An embedded (embedded) system can be defined as an autonomous electronic and computer system, which is dedicated to a specific task. Its available resources are generally limited. This limitation is generally spatial (limited size) and energetic (limited consumption).

Embedded systems very often rely on IT, especially real-time systems. The term embedded system refers to both the hardware and the software used.

## III.2. GENERAL INFORMATION ABOUT MICROCONTROLLERS

### III.2.1. HISTORY OF PROGRAMMABLE SYSTEMS

PLCs or industrial programmable systems appeared at the end of the sixties, at the request of the American automotive industry (GM), which demanded more adaptability of their control systems. The cost of electronics then made it possible to advantageously replace current technologies. Formerly using electromagnetic relays and pneumatic systems for the realization of the control parts (*wired logic*), but expensive, no flexibility, no communication possible. This is why the use of microprocessor-based systems has been resorted to, allowing easy modification of automated systems (*Programmed Logic*).

The computers of the time being expensive and not adapted to the constraints of the industrial world, the automatons or systems had to make it possible to meet the expectations of industry. [9]

From 1970 to 1974, microprocessor technology (at least the early ones) added greater flexibility and "intelligence" to programmable systems. User interface capabilities improved. The PLC or programmable system can now perform arithmetic operations in addition to logical operations; manipulate data and addresses; and communicate with other PLCs or computers, adding a new dimension to PLC applications. [10]

---

[9] *PLC course P1*
[10] *www.microcontroller/historics of microprocessor systems*

### III.2.2. PRESENTATION OF MICROPROCESSOR SYSTEMS [11]

Starting with 2300 transistors integrated in a chip in 1971 clocked at 108 kHz (<0.5 mips) (Intel 4004), today's µproc and µcontr are composed of 2 x 410,000,000 transistors clocked at 3200 Mhz for a computing power of 2 x 24,200 MiPS.

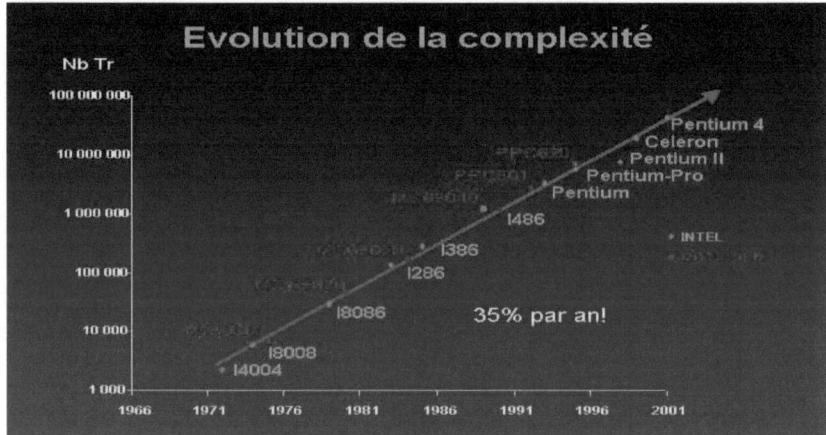

***Figure Evolution of microcontrollers***

As the fineness of the etching process allows smaller and smaller patterns, more and more transistors can be integrated per unit area. The main interest is the reduction of the size of the electronic board with more and more computing power at a constant cost.

---

[11] *Course material; microprocessor-based systems, by Thomas WATSON, President of IBM, 1943*

## III. 2.3. THE PROGRAMMING LOGIC

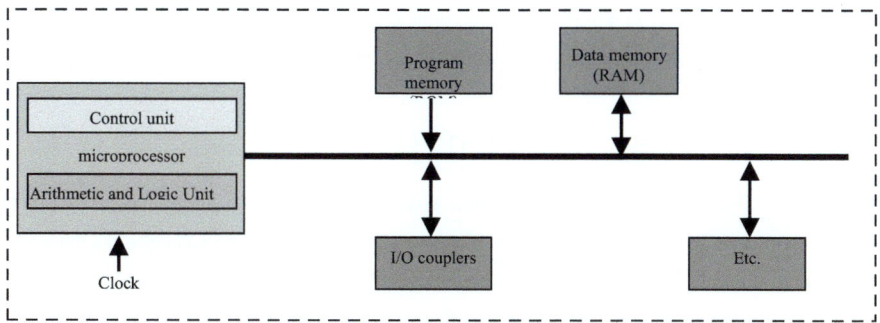

*Figure: Processor block diagrams*

## II.2.4. SIMPLIFIED STRUCTURE OF A µPROGRAMME CARD

- In wired logic, the information is processed in parallel by as many logical operators as necessary. => Limited processing complexity.
- In programmed logic, a single operator capable of performing several operations (OR, AND, +, -, x, etc.) *sequentially* processes information according to elementary orders called instructions. [12]

The microprocessor-based process is :

- The list of instructions, stored in memory
- The element capable of carrying out these instructions is the processor.
- Means to receive/transmit data interfaces or peripherals
- Electrical connections between these organs, which are the buses.
- A clock (rate of execution)

### II.2.5. DIFFERENCE BETWEEN A MICROPROCESSOR (CPU) AND A MICROCONTROLLER

One realizes integrated circuits where we find inside: CPU+RAM+ROM+I/O couplers => These circuits are called microcontrollers; whereas microprocessors need to have external elements that can only execute elementary arithmetic and logical operations defined by its instruction sets.

---

[12] *Course material; microprocessor-based systems, by Thomas WATSON, President of IBM, 1943*

**Advantages of programmed logic**

- Use of components with a high integration density: Electronic board with small footprint
- The components used are programmable: The application can be tuned or completely modified.

### III.3.INTRODUCTION TO MICROCONTROLLERS [13]

A microcontroller (abbreviated as µc, or MCU) is an integrated circuit that brings together the essential elements of a computer: processor, memories (read-only memory for the program, random access memory for data), peripheral units and input-output interfaces. Microcontrollers are characterized by a higher degree of integration, lower power consumption, lower operating speed (from a few megahertz to more than one gigahertz) and lower cost compared to the general-purpose microprocessors used in personal computers.

Compared to electronic systems based on microprocessors and other separate components, microcontrollers make it possible to reduce the size, power consumption and cost of products. They have thus made it possible to democratize the use of information technology in a large number of products and processes.

Microcontrollers are circuits with RISC (Reduce Instructions Construction Set) architecture, or reduced instruction set components. The advantage is that the smaller the number of instructions, the faster the instructions are decoded, which increases the operating speed of the microcontroller. The microcontroller family is subdivided into 3 main families :

- **The Base-Line family**: which uses 12-bit instruction words,
- **The Mid-Range family**: which uses 14-bit words, and finally
- **The High-End family**: which uses 16-bit words.

Microcontrollers are frequently used in embedded systems, such as automotive engine controllers, remote controls, office appliances, household appliances, toys, cell phones, etc. [14]

## III. 3.1. FROM MICROPROCESSOR TO MICROCONTROLLER

The processor is the central element of a computer system: it interprets the instructions and processes the data of a program. It needs certain external elements to function:

---

[13] the PIC10F200 [archive] from Micro chip works at 4 MHz, the LPC 3131 [archive] from NXP works at 180 MHz

[14] Part 1: Microcontrollers ( micro chip peaks )

- A clock to clock it (usually quartz or Phase Locked Loop (PLL));
- Memory to store variables during program execution (RAM RAM) and the program from one power-up to the next (ROM). If you design a system assigned to a particular task (which is usually the case for embedded systems), the program does not have to change. It can therefore be stored in a read-only memory (ROM);
- Peripherals (to interact with the outside world).

These elements are connected by 3 buses :

- The address bus that allows the microprocessor to select the memory box or the device it wants to access to read or write information (instruction or data) ;
- The data bus which allows the transfer of information between the different elements; this information will be either instructions or data from or to the memory or peripherals ;
- The control bus that indicates whether the current operation is a read or write, whether a device requests an interrupt to send information back to the processor, etc.

Traditionally, these components are integrated into separate circuits. The development of such a microprocessor-based system is therefore penalized by (non-exhaustive list) :

- The need to provide for the interconnection of these components (bus, cabling, connection layers) ;
- The space physically occupied by the components and the means of interconnection ;
- Energy consumption ;
- The heat released ;
- The financial cost.

Microcontrollers improve the integration and cost (related to design and implementation) of a microprocessor-based system by bringing these essential elements together in a single integrated circuit. A microcontroller is therefore a stand-alone component, capable of executing the program contained in its read-only memory as soon as it is powered up. Depending on the model and operating conditions, microcontrollers may require some external components (quartz, some capacitors, sometimes a ROM), but this is very limited.

When *all* the functions of the computer system are grouped in a single integrated circuit, including logic, analog, radio frequency, interface functions (USB, Ethernet, etc.), then we speak of System *on Chip* (*system on a chip* or *single-chip system*). These components are based on one or more cores of microcontroller, microprocessor, graphics processor, DSP, device controller, etc....

### III.3.2. MICROCONTROLLERS (MICROCHIP)

### III.3.3.INTEREST OF MICROCONTROLLERS [15]

Microcontrollers are so small that they can be easily implanted in the very application they are supposed to control.

Their price and performance greatly simplify the design of electronic and computer systems.

We can still specify :

- The performances are identical or even superior to its competitors.
- Widely used so very available.
- The development tools are free and downloadable from the web.
- The reduced instruction set is flexible, powerful and easy to master.
- The versions with flash memory offer flexibility and practical advantages.

The user community is very present on the web. The use of microcontrollers is only limited by the ingenuity of the designers, they can be found in our coffee makers, VCRs, radios, etc ...


### III.3.4. SOME MICROCONTROLLERS

A microcontroller executes instructions. The "instruction cycle" is defined as the time required to execute an instruction. Be careful not to confuse this notion with the clock cycle, which corresponds to the time needed to execute an elementary operation (i.e. a clock stroke).

An instruction is executed in two phases :

- The phase of searching for the binary code of the instruction stored in the program memory
- The execution phase or code of the instruction is interpreted by the processor and executed.

Each instruction cycle lasts 4 clock strokes as shown in the following figure :

---

[15] V. Tourtchine. Microcontroller of the PIC family. Course material & MPLAB software

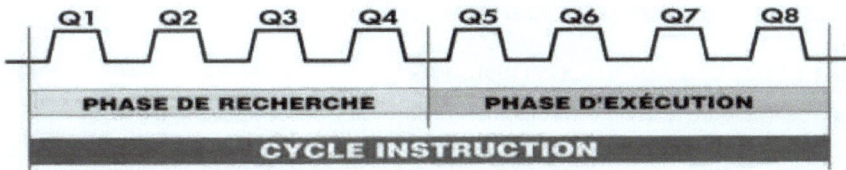

*Figure: Instruction cycle*

## III.4 MICROCONTROLLER OVERVIEW

### III.4.1.FAMILY OF MICROCONTROLLERS [16]

There are several microcontrollers of different families among which we quote :

### III4.1.1 PIC

A PIC microcontroller is a unit for processing and executing information to which internal peripherals have been added, allowing assemblies to be made without the need for additional components. A PIC microcontroller can therefore operate autonomously after programming.

PICs integrate non-volatile program memory (FLASH), volatile data memory (SRAM), non-volatile data memory (E2PROM), input/output ports (digital, analog, Timers, etc.), and even a clock, although external time bases can be used. Some models have USB and Ethernet ports and processing units.

The name PIC is not officially an acronym, although translation to "Peripheral Interface Controller" is generally accepted. However, at the time of the development of PIC1650 by General Instrument. PIC was an acronym for Programmable Intelligent Computer or Programmable Integrated Circuit.

---

[16] *Wikibooks: Using theHow to get started with a PIC16F84,PIC16cxxx/16fxxx family peakPIC 16F and 18F, on Wikiversity*

### III.4.1.1.1. ARCHITECTURE

PICs conform to the Harvard architecture: they have separate program memory and data memory. Most instructions occupy one word of program memory. The size of these words depends on the PIC model, while the data memory is organized in bytes.

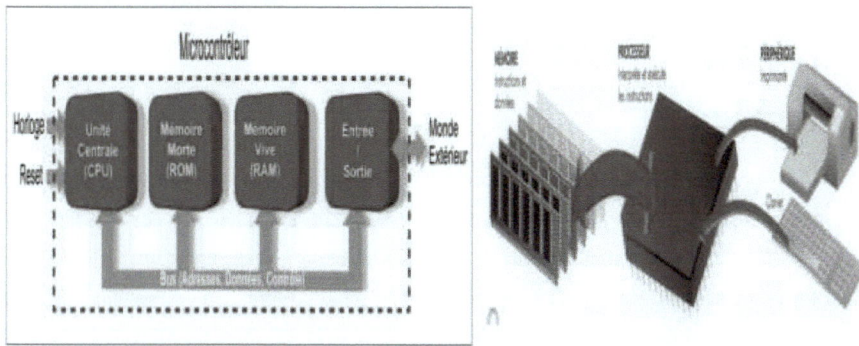

Figure

PICs are so-called RISC processors, i.e. a processor with a reduced instruction set. The smaller the number of instructions, the easier and faster the decoding is, and the faster the component works. However, more instructions are needed to perform a complex operation.

The number of clock cycles (Tosc) per instruction cycle (Tcy) depends on the architecture of the PIC: Tcy=4*Tosc (8 bits), Tcy=2*Tosc (16bits), Tcy=Tosc (32 bits). As most instructions are executed in a single cycle, except for jumps, this gives a power of the order of 1 MIPS per MHz (1 million instructions per second).

PICs can be clocked at 20/32 MHz (PIC16/PIC16F1 series), 40/48/64 MHz (PIC18/PIC18"J"/PIC18"K" series), 80/100(PIC32MX), 120/200 (PIC32MZ).

The 10F and 12F family: These are recent components. They have the particularities of being extremely small (to give an idea, they exist in SOT-23 6-pin package of less than 3×3 mm), simple and economical.

- ThePIC14F family: Intermediate range between PIC16 and PIC18. This range is no longer enriched by Micro chip. It supports C compilation.
- The 16F family: The PICs of the 16C or 16F family are mid-range components. It is the richest family in terms of derivatives.

  The 16F Family now has 3 sub-families:
  - The subfamily with the Baseline core: 12-bit instructions (PIC16Fxxx)
  - The subfamily with the Middle-Range core: 14-bit instructions (PIC16Fxxx)
  - The subfamily with the Enhanced core: 14-bit instructions (PIC16F1xxx)

### III.4.1.2. ARDUINO

### III.4.1.2.1. HISTORY

In 2005, a project whose consequences nobody had imagined was launched at the Interactive Design Institute Ivrea, in Ivrea, Italy. A prototyping plate was developed to give students a simple way to design innovative products. One name keeps coming up in this context, that of Massimo Banzi. He is one of the co-developers and co-founders of Arduino LLC. For the anecdote, the name *Arduino* was borrowed from a bar in Ivrea where the project's instigators regularly met.

The philosophy behind the whole affair is to simplify and facilitate access to the world of electronics and microcontrollers so that everyone can use it without being a specialist in these fields. The high availability and low cost of the Arduino board, as well as the electronic components and modules, also contributed to the board's rapid popularity.

Digital I/O

Microcontroller

Button of
reset

Entries
analog

USB socket

Food

Power outlet

### III.4.1.2.2. DATA PROCESSING UNIT (ATMEGA 328P)

The high-performance RISC micro chip pico Power 8-bit microcontroller combines 32KB ISP flash memory with read-write capabilities, EEPROM 1024B, SRAM 2KB, 23 general purpose I/O lines, 32 versatile working registers, three flexible timers / counters with comparison modes, internal and external switches, programmable serial USART, byte-oriented 2-wire serial interface, SPI serial port, 6-channel 10-bit A/D converter (8 channels in TQFP and QFN/MLF packages), programmable monitoring timer with internal oscillator and five software selectable power saving modes. The unit operates between 1.8-5.5 volts[17] . The use of the ATMega 328p meets the needs has a data processing unit received from the RFID reader (ID employee, transmit the information to the database via the attached USB cable).

---

17 ATmega328 - 8-bit AVR Microcontrollers - Microcontrollers and Processors ". [Online]. Available on: https://www.microchip.com/wwwproducts/en/ATmega328.

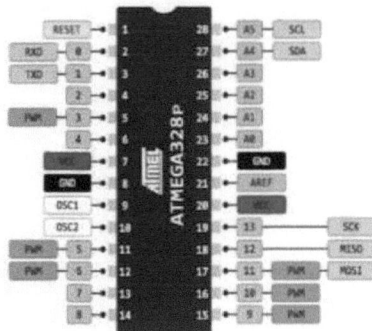

Figure II-4 ATMega 328p microcontrollers

| FEATURES | VALUE |
|---|---|
| Type of program memory | Flash |
| Program memory size (KB) | 32 |
| Processor speed (MIPS / DMIPS) | 20 |
| SRAM Bytes | 2 048 |
| EEPROM / HEF data (bytes) | 1024 |
| Digital Communication Devices | 1-UART, 2-SPI, 1-I2C |
| Capture / compare / PWM devices | 1 input capture, 1 CCP, 6PWM |
| Timers | 2 x 8 bits, 1 x 16 bits |
| Number of comparators | 1 |
| Temperature range (C) | -40 à 85 |
| Operating voltage range (V) | 1,8 à 5,5 |
| Number of pins | 32 |
| Low battery | Yes |

Table II-4 Data sheets of the ATMega-328p. [18]

[18] ATmega328 - 8-bit AVR Microcontrollers - Microcontrollers and Processors ". [Online]. Available on: https://www.microchip.com/wwwproducts/en/ATmega328.

The microcontroller is pre-programmed with a boot loader so that a dedicated programmer is not required.

The modules are programmed with a TTL serial connection, but the connections for this programming differ between models. The first Arduino had an RS-232 serial port, then USB appeared on the Diecimila models, while some modules intended for portable use such as the Lillypad or the Pro-mini freed themselves from the programming interface, relocated on a dedicated USB-serial module (in the form of a card or cable), this also allowed to reduce their cost, the USB-Serial TTL converter (an FTDI232RL from FTDI) costing quite a lot.

The Arduino uses most of the inputs/outputs of the microcontroller for interfacing with the other circuits. The Diecimila model, for example, has fourteen digital inputs/outputs, six of which can produce PWM signals, and six analog inputs. Connections are made through HE14 female connectors located on the top of the board, with expansion modules stacked on top of the Arduino. Several kinds of extensions are commercially available.

Other cards like the Arduino Nano or the Pro micro use male connectors, allowing to place them on an experimental board.

STMicroelectronics also worked with Arduino on compatible boards. The STM32 Nucleo boards, based on STM32 processors, use the ARM architecture rather than the Harvard architecture of the Atmel AVRs. These boards feature a more powerful processor, ARM Cortex M 32-bit, from M0+ at 32 MHz or M0 at 48 MHz up to M4 at 100 MHz, with DSP instructions[19] and a Chrom-ART graphics processor from STMicroelectronics[20].

### III.4.1.2.3. STRUCTURE OF AN ARDUINO PROGRAM [21]

Arduino programs are developed in a clean development environment based on C and C++. An Arduino program is called "sketch" and has a special structure (see figure 2). Such a sketch consists of three blocks :

- The block of declarations and initializations. In this block, external C/C++ libraries can be integrated if necessary by means of the include statement;

---

[19]*développez.net : Discovery of the STM32 Nucleo card*
*20 Pierrick Arlot, ST's STM32 microcontrollers jump into the Arduino universe, on L'Embarqué, May 20, 2016*
*21 Http://www.data scheet arduino.com*

- The second block corresponds to the setup function (). The setup function () is usually used to program the individual pins of the microcontroller. This defines which pins are to be used as inputs and outputs. Some of them are connected to sensors, push buttons or temperature-sensitive resistors, which bring signals from the outside to a specific input of the microcontroller. Others lead signals to outputs to control specific equipment.
- The third block corresponds to the loop () function. The loop () function forms an endless loop, by means of which sensors are interrogated and pre-actuators are continuously controlled.

Apart from these three blocks, it is possible to develop as many functions or objects as one wishes according to the logic of the problem to be solved. These functions and objects are used in the loop() function. We find the structure of the programs described below:

*Figure   : IDE of Arduino*

38

### III.4.1.3. RASPBERRY

### III.4.1.3.1. HISTORY [22]

In 2006 the first prototypes of the Raspberry Pi are developed on Atmel ATmega 644 microcontrollers. The schematic and PCB layout are made public. This computer is inspired by Acorn Computer's BBC Micro (1981) and is intended to encourage young people to take up programming. The first ARM prototype is integrated in a box the same size as a USB stick with a USB port on one side and an HDMI port on the other.

The foundation's objective is then to offer two versions, one at US$25 and a second at US$35.

The opening of orders for model B (most expensive) took place on February 29, 2012 and on February 4, 2013 for model A (least expensive).

Raspberry Pi is a small computer under the Linux operating system on SD card for embedded computing applications. The heart of the computer is an FPGA (Broadcom 2835) with a 700MHz ARM11 processor and many peripherals.

Raspberry Pi can be directly connected to a conventional HMI, HDMI mouse/keyboard/screen or composite video, however like any Linux computer, Raspberry Pi can integrate its own development tools and a SSH-based human-machine interface that can be controlled from another computer via Ethernet or WIFI.

The expansion connector supports parallel inputs/outputs as well as most communication buses. It is a particularly economical and powerful medium that can be easily

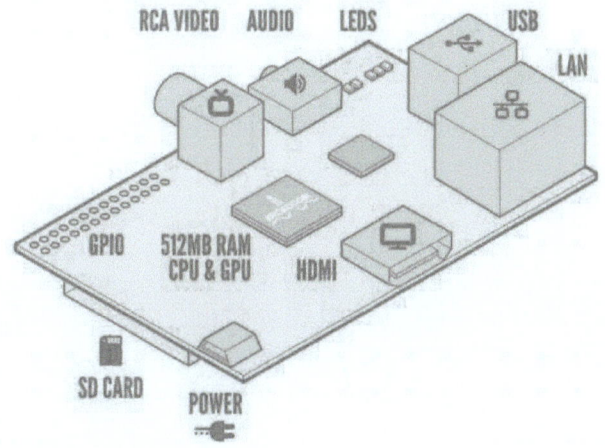

[22] http://www.raspberrypi.org/archives/3215

implemented in small systems requiring access to the physical world by sensors/actuators with digital interfaces.

## III.4.1.3.2. THE RASPERRY EXTENSION CONNECTOR PI [23]

Most of the TPs use the extension connector of the Raspberry Pi card. It is necessary to wire the peripherals correctly on this connector.

---

[23] *http://www.raspberrypi.org/*

### III.4.1.3.3. GPIO CONNECTOR

The GPIO connector supports GPIOs (binary inputs/outputs) but also PWM outputs, communication peripherals (UART, I2C, SPI) and 5v and 3V3 power supplies. The pins can have different functions depending on whether they are activated as GPIO or communication device. Some of them have pull-up resistors giving a dominant 0 bit and a recessive 1 bit. Ex I2C)

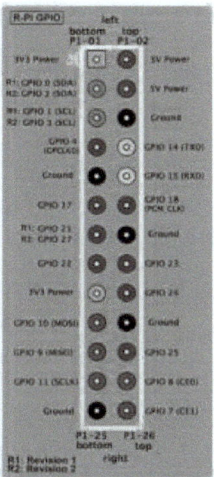

# CHAPTER IV. IMPLEMENTATION OF THE AUTOMATIC POINTING SYSTEM

## IV.1 INTRODUCTION

In this chapter, we will first present the project and the different materials selected for its realization; then we will move on to the step that consists in realizing an automatic presence system based on contactless radio identification (RFID). Each employee (staff) receives a unique identification card used for his authentication, it allows to know the personal information and the validation heur in the system to manage either presence and access in the company premises.

Mainly in our work we have focused much more on employee attendance management, for the other functions it only takes a few changes in the same database to give or restrict access to other types of accounts.

## IV.2 PRESENTATION OF THE PROJECT

From a global perspective, the deployment of the RFID pointing system will benefit human resources management, as the presence of employees in the workplace is one of the key factors in improving productivity and monitoring the performance of each of them.

This chapter is divided into two main parts, the first part of which will present various electronic tools, and the second part will present the IT part and the realization of the project.

## IV. 2.1. PRESENTATION OF ELECTRONIC TOOLS

We are going to use for the realization of our project different electronic equipment which is essential thanks to their simplicity, efficiency, low cost and at least their availability. We mention an Arduino board (Arduino Uno with an ATmega 328 P microcontroller), a RFID Kit composed of a reader (@13 kHz) and some RFID tags (Cards + Tags), a USB cable to ensure serial connectivity between the Arduino board and the processing center, LEDs, etc. ... In what follows we will proceed to present in detail the elements used to design and build the complete system.

### IV. 2.1.1. ARDUINO CARDS
This map was presented in the previous chapter.

### IV.2.1.2. THE RFID LABEL (TAG)

Also known as a smart label, smart tag or tag is an electronic identification medium that does not need to be seen to be read. Its use is therefore very attractive to meet traceability requirements. The RFID label is the most used RFID support, it consists in sheltering a serial number or a series of data on a chip connected to an antenna.

The label is activated by a radio signal emitted by the RFID reader itself equipped with a RFID card and an antenna, the labels transmit the data they contain in return.
24

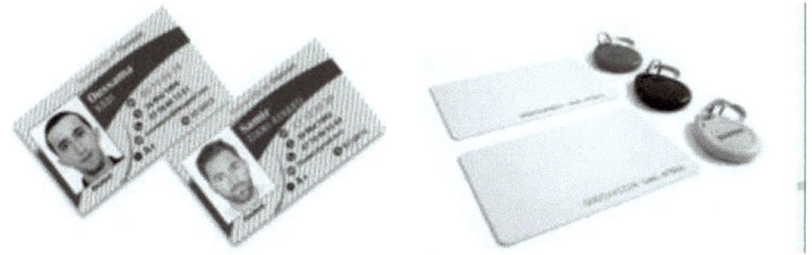

Figure II-2 RFID Tag

### IV.2.1.3. THE RFID READER

The RFID reader (Figure II-3) is like an Arduino module under the name RC522, it allows contactless identification of RFID tags as it is already explained in the first chapter. It is based on the Philips RC522 integrated circuit. It uses the ISM [25]13.56MHz band, the communication distance can go up to 6cm, but most NFC modules work very well with 1cm distance. The features of this RC522 module are :

- Low voltage, 3.3V, current   13-25mA
- Low cost
- Simple to implement with Arduino boards and all microcontrollers
- Frequency of use      : 13.56MHz, the FIFO buffer manages 64 bytes Rx/Tx.
- SPI interface.
- Working temperature -25 ~ 85 °C.

---

24 K. Finkenzeller, Fundamentals and applications in contactless smart cards, radio frequency identification and nearfield communication, 3rd ed. Chichester, West Sussex ; Hoboken, NJ: Wiley, 2010.
[25] ISM : Industrial - Scientific - Medical

- Small and very light size (71.00mm × 40.90mm) which allows its integration without cluttering up the other components of the printed circuit board.
- On the other hand, the reading distance is limited to 6 cm to ensure a good reading of

the tag.

Figure II-3 the RFID Reader (RC 522)

| TYPE | SYMBOL | DESCRIPTION |
|---|---|---|
| | 3.3v | VCC |
| | RST | Reset |
| | GND | Ground |
| The pins | IRQ | Interrupt request |
| | MISO | SPI interface |
| | MOSI | SPI interface |
| | SCK | SPI interface |
| | SS | Slave selection |

Table II-1 Description of the MFRC522 Pins

## IV2.2. PRESENTATION OF COMPUTER TOOLS

### IV.2.2.1. ARDUINO IDE

The Arduino software (IDE) [26]is a development environment based on the C language used to upload and compile programs into Arduino cards. It is a free and open source software, available for download from the official Arduino website. It exists in different platforms namely Windows, Linux and Mac OS.

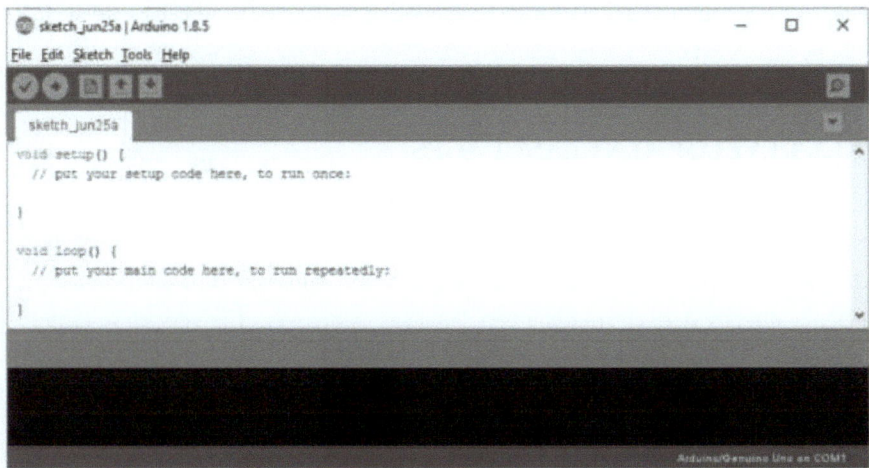

Figure II-5 the main interface of Arduino IDE

### IV.2.2.2 DATABASE MANAGEMENT

- **Microsoft SQL Server** is a database management system (DBMS) in SQL language incorporating among others a RDBMS (relational DBMS ") developed and marketed by Microsoft. It runs under Windows and Linux OS (since March 2016), but it is possible to launch it on Mac OS via Docker, because there is a version available for download on the Microsoft website. [27]

- **SQL schema** management The flexibility of SQL schema management is such that it is possible to transfer an object from one schema to another simply by using an ALTER SCHEMA command. The owners are distinct from the schemas and it is possible to transfer

---

*26 Arduino - Software ". [Online]. Available at: https://www.arduino.cc/en/Main/Software?*

*27 https://docs.microsoft.com/en-us/sql/linux/quickstart-install-connect-docker*

the ownership of a database, a schema or an object from one SQL user to another, through the ALTER AUTHORIZATION command.

- SQL Server **parallelism** works natively in parallel. As soon as a query is estimated to exceed the cost threshold at which a query plan can be parallelized, SQL Server rewrites the plan using multi-threaded algorithms and if the new plan proves to be less expensive, the substitution takes place automatically. This functionality exists in all editions and is not a paid module to be added in addition as it is the case with Oracle. The physical read and write operations also benefit from the systematic parallelism of the IO operations being carried out directly by SQL Server and not through the system layer as is the case with PostgreSQL or MySQL.

### IV.2.2.3. DEVELOPMENT LANGUAGES

- C# pronounced "C-Sharp" is an object-oriented programming language. It is marketed by the American company Microsoft since 2002 and is used to develop on the .NET platform (pronounced "dot net"). As its name indicates, this programming language is directly derived from the C++ language. Moreover, it is very close to the Java language, it includes the main concepts as well as the syntax by adding certain notions (operator overchanging, delegates, indexers...). If the language used alone remains rather limited, the use of this language supplemented by the .NET Framework offers many possibilities (creation and opening of windows, network access, use of databases).

This language can also be used to create web applications using the ASP.NET platform. C# is currently a highly valued skill in business and is increasingly seen as a competitor to the Java language.

- **C#, a high-level language**

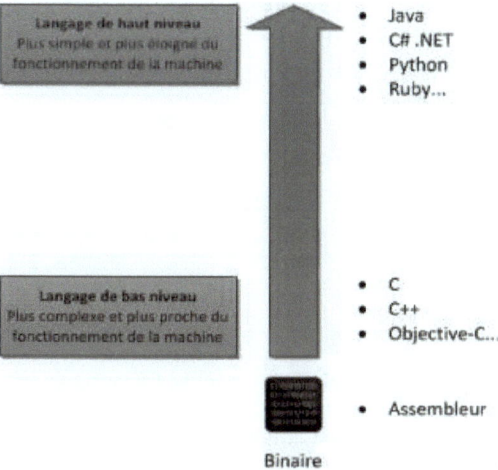

Figure II-6 Programming language

Languages are classified into two categories, they are said to be **low level** or **high level**.

A so-called high-level language is a language quite far from binary (and therefore from the way the machine works), which generally allows for more flexible and rapid development.

In contrast to high-level language, low-level language is closer to how the machine works: it usually requires a little more effort but also gives you more control over what you do.

As opposed to C and C++ and despite its name, C# is therefore considered a high-level language. This language is closer to Java in its use and versatility.

- **Characteristics of the C# language**

Of course, C# being an object-oriented language, it is therefore possible to use the following concepts:

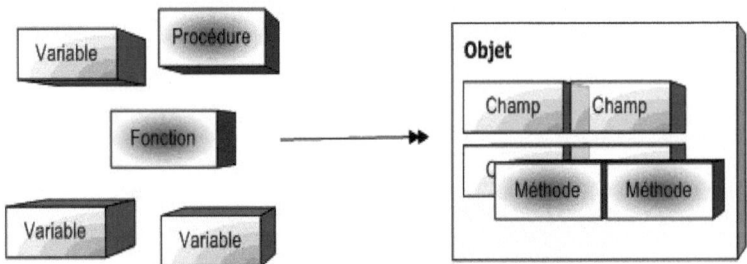

Figure II.7. Characteristic of the C# language

- **Encapsulation**: Encapsulation allows to gather data and methods within a structure by hiding the implementation of the object. In this way it is impossible to access the data by any other means than the services offered. Encapsulation thus makes it possible to guarantee the integrity of the data contained in the object.

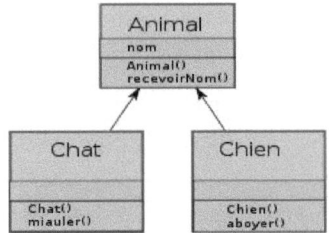

Figure II-8 Encapsulation

- **Inheritance**: When declaring a new class, it is possible to include all the characteristics of another class, then called **parent class**. It is thus said that the newly created class (called **"daughter class"**) inherits from the mother class. This is a very powerful process, specific to object language, being one of the main strengths of this kind of language. In the example above the classes "Cat" and "Dog" are the daughter classes that inherit from the parent class "Animal". Both have the attribute "Name" and the method "receiveName()". Each one has its own method "meow()" or "bark()".

- **Polymorphism**: there are 3 types of polymorphism. The first is called **ad hoc polymorphism**, so it is possible in any object-oriented language to have 2 totally

48

different objects but having a method of the same name and acting differently. The second type is called **parametric polymorphism**, so an object can have several methods of the same name but with different parameters in number and/or type. This makes it possible to automatically choose the right method to adopt according to the type of data passed in parameter. 3rd and last type, the **inheritance polymorphism** which allows daughter class objects to redefine one or more methods in order to change their behavior. If we look further than these basic principles of object-oriented programming, we can see that C# has its own assets that differ from other languages:

- **Delegates**: allow to create special variables. These are variables pointing to a method. Acting like function pointers in C and C++, these delegates are much more precise due to the C# language which is much more typed.

- **Properties** that can replace getters and setters for private attributes.

- **LINQ (Language Integrated Query)** allows the SQL-like way of querying, filtering and projecting data into collections, enumerable classes, databases or even other data sources. The only requirement is that this data is stored in objects.

Unlike C, C++ and Java, C# is much more flexible. There are no separate header files, and types and methods do not have to be declared in any particular order. A C# source file can define any number of classes, interfaces and events.

## IV.2.2.4. PROTEUS DESIGN

Proteus Design [28]is a complete software suite for the design and simulation of printed circuit boards. It includes several modules such as Firmware IDE and PCB Layout to create the circuit mask; which appears as tabs in the same integrated application. It contains a complete and open component library. This provides a smooth and responsive workflow for the electronics engineer.

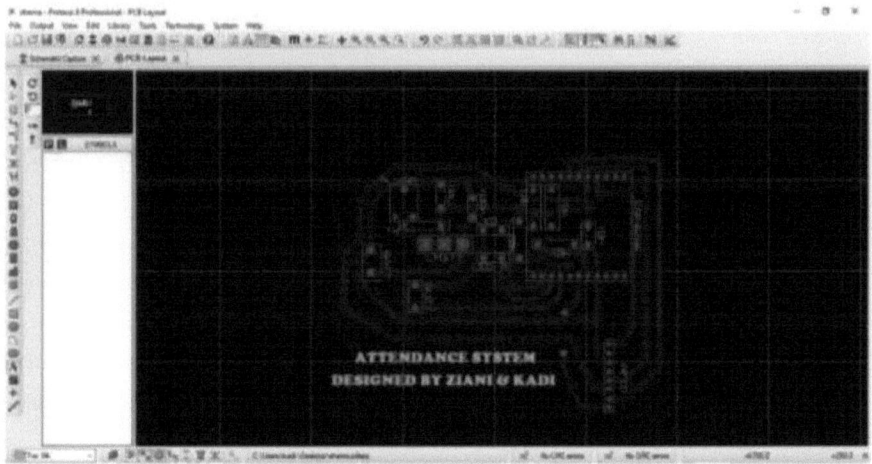

Figure II-9 the environment Proteus ARES [29]

[28] *Proteus - PCB Design, Layout & Simulation software - Labcenter Electronics ". [Online]. Available at: https://www.labcenter.com/.*
[29] *Proteus - PCB Design, Layout & Simulation software - Labcenter Electronics ". [Online]. Available at: https://www.labcenter.com/.*

## IV.3. ORGANIZATION CHART

The flowchart shown in Figure II-10 shows the flow of the system, as soon as a card is detected (Service Card), the identifier of this card is read and converted from Hex to Decimal. It is then checked in the database (SQL Server) and if it is there, the opening mechanism of the input protection is activated; the transfer of the id is done from the RC522 reader (RFID) to the microcontroller via the serial interface (bit-by-bit serial protocol); then, to the database server via the USB cable.

If successful, a green light (LED) is lit followed by a validation beep (buzzer); otherwise a red light is lit followed by a buzz.

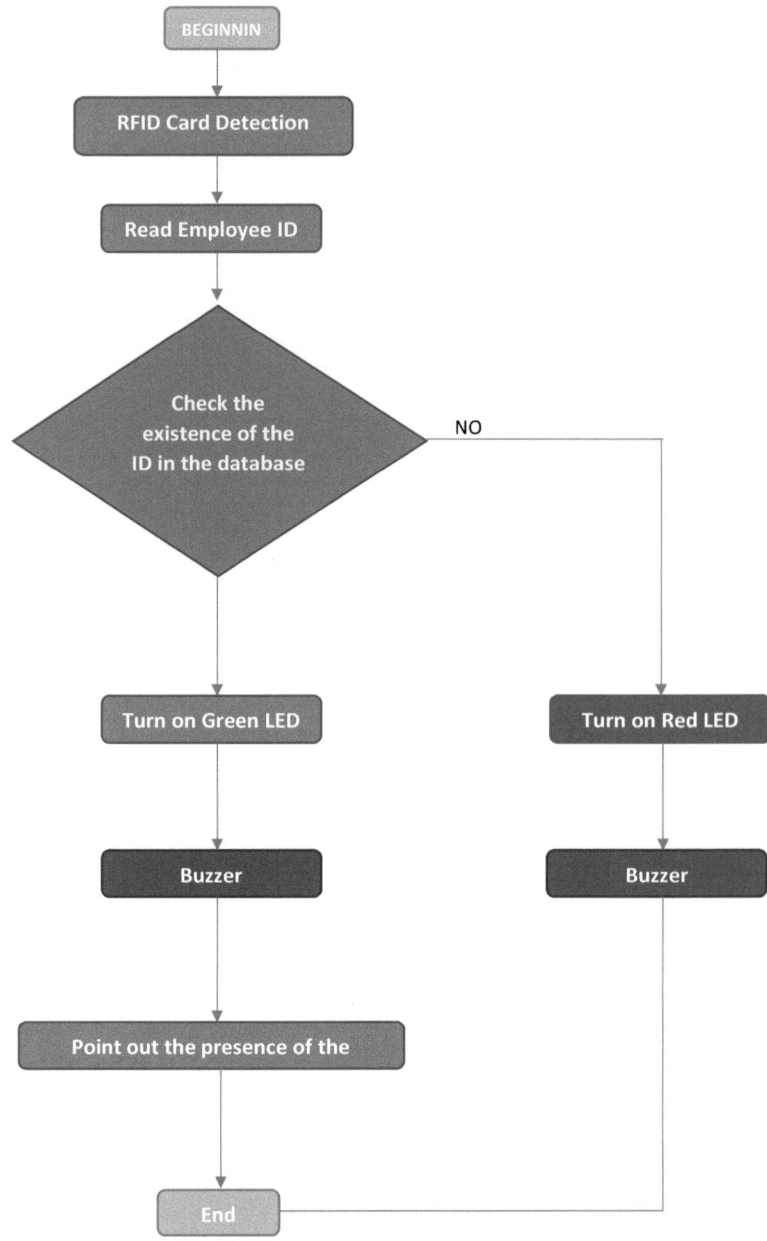

Figure II-10 Project flowcharts

## II.10. Conclusion

In this chapter, we have highlighted the phases necessary for the realization of our project by describing the different hardware and software tools for the realization of the said project. We have broken down our work into two parts: Electronics and Computer Science.

In the computer part. We presented the different software that allowed us to develop the database as well as the business logic of the project.

In the electronic part, the different components and modules and their characteristics were mentioned. The next chapter will be dedicated to the elaboration and realization of the Automatic Pointing System.

## IV.4. PROJECT IMPLEMENTATION

### IV.4.1. CREATION OF THE DATABASE

To mark the presence of employees, a database containing information about each employee will be needed. It contains tables such as (Agents, Functions, Departments, Scores, User...). Figure III-1 shows a capture of the main Microsoft SQL Management Studio interface.

To create a new table, you need sufficient access to the data (user name ;

Password) and hardware resources (access to the database administrator's server PCs).

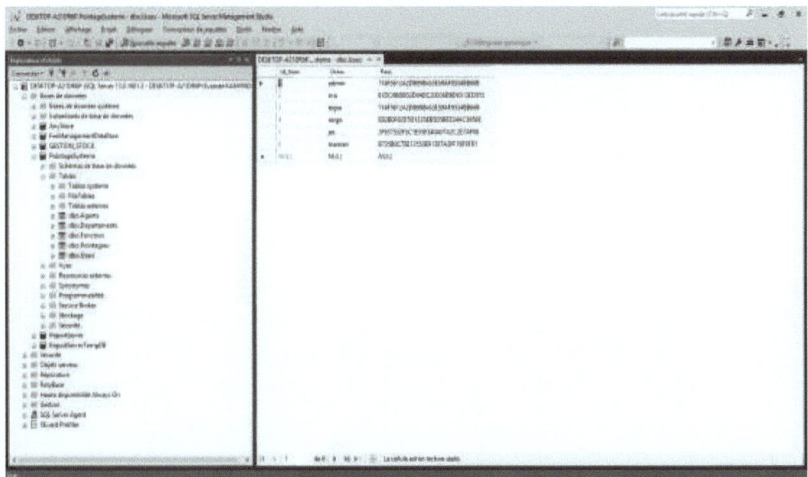

Figure III-1 Microsoft SQL Management Studio main interface

The relationships between the different tables are shown in the following diagram :

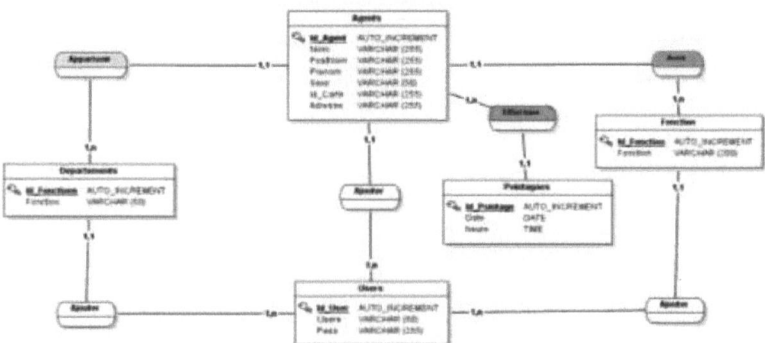

Figure III-2 Application Database Designation

54

## IV.4.2. CREATION OF THE USER INTERFACE

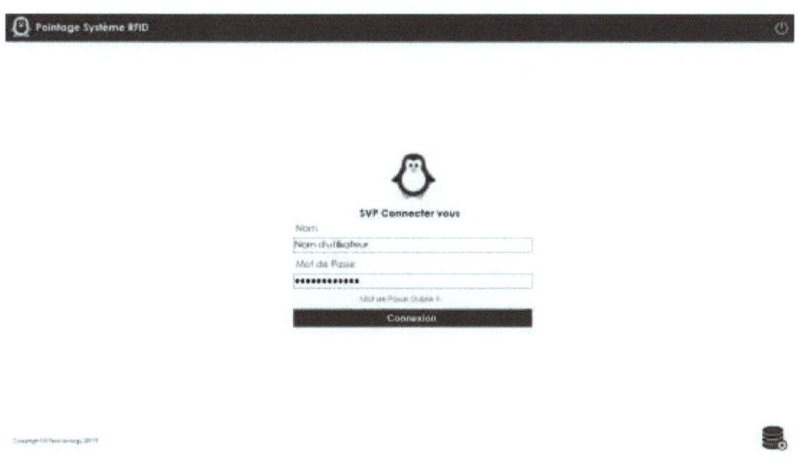

**Figure IV.1 Connection window**

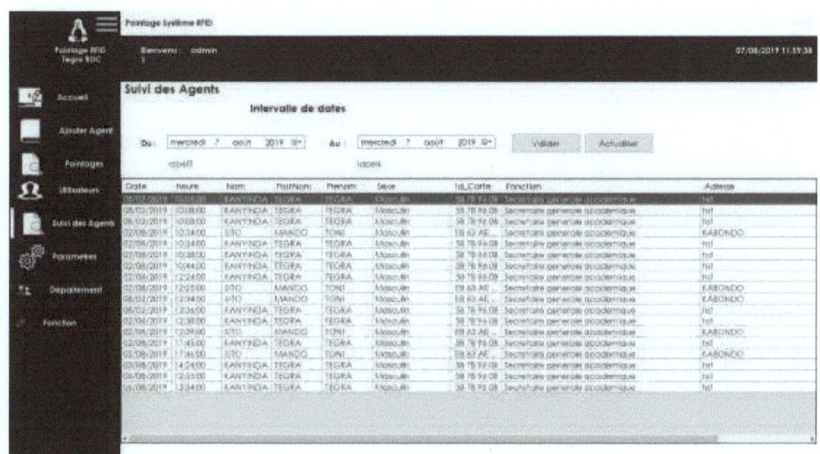

**IV.2 Agent tracking window**